CATS SET I

TABBY CATS

Tamara L. Britton
ABDO Publishing Company

Published by ABDO Publishing Company, 8000 West 78th Street, Edina, Minnesota 55439. Copyright © 2011 by Abdo Consulting Group, Inc. International copyrights reserved in all countries. No part of this book may be reproduced in any form without written permission from the publisher. The Checkerboard Library™ is a trademark and logo of ABDO Publishing Company.

Printed in the United States of America, North Mankato, Minnesota.
042010
092010

 PRINTED ON RECYCLED PAPER

Cover Photo: Peter Arnold
Interior Photos: Photo by Helmi Flick pp. 5, 7, 9, 10, 11;
    iStockphoto pp. 8, 13, 15, 16, 17, 19; Peter Arnold p. 21

Editor: BreAnn Rumsch
Art Direction & Cover Design: Neil Klinepier

Library of Congress Cataloging-in-Publication Data

Britton, Tamara L., 1963-
  Tabby cats / Tamara L. Britton.
      p. cm. -- (Cats)
  Includes index.
  ISBN 978-1-61613-402-0
  1. Tabby cats--Juvenile literature. I. Title.
  SF449.T32B75 2011
  636.8--dc22
                                2010014961

CONTENTS

Lions, Tigers, and Cats 4

Tabby Cats 6

Qualities 8

Coat and Color 10

Size 12

Care 14

Feeding 16

Kittens 18

Buying a Kitten 20

Glossary 22

Web Sites 23

Index 24

Lions, Tigers, and Cats

Cats have been valued human companions for centuries. This relationship began in ancient Africa. About 3,500 years ago, Egyptians began taming African wildcats. These cats hunted rats and mice that feasted on stored grain harvests.

Modern **domestic** cats can trace their roots back to these African wildcats. Cats are cherished as family pets. Today, more than 40 different **breeds** of domestic cats exist worldwide.

The family **Felidae** includes 37 different species. Domestic cats are members of this family. Lions and tigers belong to this family, too!

A tabby cat

TABBY CATS

Though there are more than 40 different cat **breeds**, tabby is not one of them! Tabby is a type of coat coloring. All cats with this coat type are called tabby cats.

The tabby coat comes from the **domestic** cat's African wildcat ancestors. The coat patterns provided the camouflage these cats needed to survive in the wild. Today, the tabby coat occurs in many different cat breeds.

A tabby cat can be recognized by the M-shaped pattern on its forehead. This marking is known as the Tabby M.

QUALITIES

A tabby cat's qualities are associated with its **breed**. Many tabby cats are mixed-breed cats. These working cats catch mice in homes and barns. They make good house cats and companion animals.

This tabby house cat keeps her backyard free of mice!

Other tabby cats are **purebred** cats. Brown tabby is the most popular Maine coon cat color. This heavy-coated breed is affectionate

This tabby Persian is a famous show cat.

and loyal. Maine coons are excellent mousers, love people, and like to play.

The active Cornish Rex cat maintains its kittenish nature throughout its life. This **breed**'s short, wavy coat comes in a variety of tabby colors.

The Persian cat is the most popular breed recognized by the **Cat Fanciers' Association**. It has a sweet, gentle personality and a long, fluffy coat. Tabby Persians come in so many colors they have their own group within the breed!

COAT AND COLOR

There are four types of tabby patterns. Each has different markings. Parallel stripes line the sides of a mackerel tabby. A classic tabby displays swirl patterns on its sides. Spots make the spotted tabby stand out. The **ticked** tabby does not have stripes, swirls, or spots. It has tabby markings on its face and tail.

SILVER SPOTTED

RED MACKEREL

10

Tabby patterns come in many colors. A brown tabby has black markings on a brown or gray coat. A tabby with gray markings on a lighter gray or **buff** coat is called blue. The recognizable red tabby has orange markings on a cream coat.

A cream tabby has cream markings on a pale cream coat. A silver tabby can have black, blue, cream, or red markings. Yet, it always has a white coat.

A tabby cat's eye color depends on its coat color. Its eyes can be blue, gold, green, or hazel.

BROWN TICKED

SILVER CLASSIC

SIZE

A tabby's size depends its **breed**. For example, the brown tabby Maine coon cat is large and muscular. Males range from 12 to 18 pounds (5 to 8 kg). Females are smaller. They weigh between 9 and 12 pounds (4 and 5 kg).

The silver tabby Egyptian Mau is medium sized. Males of this breed weigh between 7 and 12 pounds (3 and 5 kg). Females range from 6 to 8 pounds (2.5 to 4 kg).

A red tabby Persian is a smaller breed. Males range from 6 to 9 pounds (2.5 to 4 kg). Females weigh between 5 and 7 pounds (2 and 3 kg).

This brown tabby Maine coon cat kitten has a long way to grow. In 2006, the world's largest cat was a Maine coon that weighed 35 pounds (16 kg)!

CARE

Cats are naturally clean animals. They spend a lot of time grooming their fur with their rough tongues. Tabby cats with short coats can easily keep their fur clean.

Tabbies with longer coats will need some help. They should be brushed regularly to remove loose hair. This will keep a cat from forming hairballs in its stomach.

Cats also have a natural instinct to bury their waste. So, you can train your tabby cat to use a **litter box**. Put the box in a quiet place away from the cat's food and water. Do not forget to remove waste from the box daily!

Like their wildcat ancestors, tabby cats are natural hunters. They do well exploring the outdoors. There, they sharpen their claws on trees.

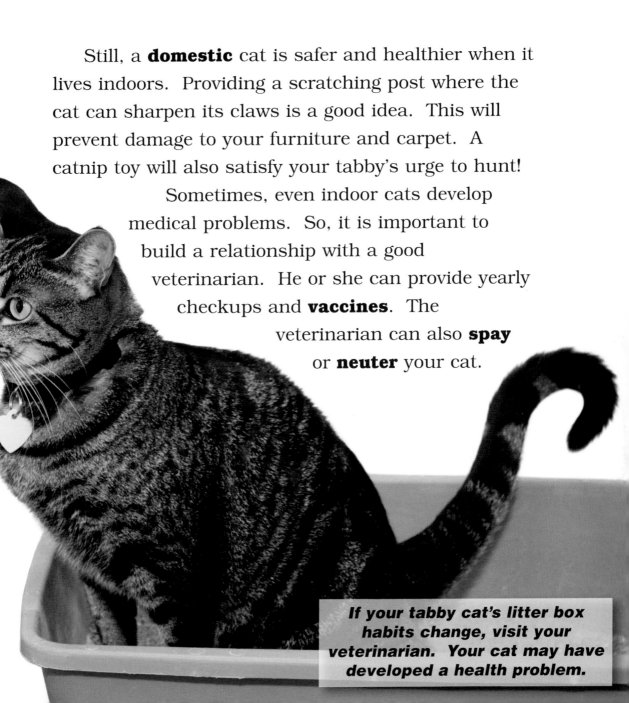

Still, a **domestic** cat is safer and healthier when it lives indoors. Providing a scratching post where the cat can sharpen its claws is a good idea. This will prevent damage to your furniture and carpet. A catnip toy will also satisfy your tabby's urge to hunt!

Sometimes, even indoor cats develop medical problems. So, it is important to build a relationship with a good veterinarian. He or she can provide yearly checkups and **vaccines**. The veterinarian can also **spay** or **neuter** your cat.

If your tabby cat's litter box habits change, visit your veterinarian. Your cat may have developed a health problem.

FEEDING

Cats are carnivores by nature. So they need a source of protein in their diets such as fish, beef, or chicken. Commercial cat food usually contains all the **nutrients** a cat needs.

There are three kinds of commercial cat food. They are dry, semimoist, and canned. Read the label to find the food best suited to your cat's needs. The label will

Kittens need to eat several times a day. Cats can be fed once or twice a day.

16

tell you how much to feed your pet based on its age, weight, and health.

In addition to healthy food, a tabby cat needs plenty of fresh water. Make sure to have some available at all times.

Tabbies also like treats. But don't be too generous! Indoor cats can easily become overweight. If your cat's weight concerns you, your veterinarian can recommend a healthy feeding schedule.

Do not let your cat become overweight!

KITTENS

At 7 to 12 months of age, tabby cats are able to reproduce. After mating, a female is **pregnant** for about 63 to 65 days. The size of her **litter** depends on her **breed**. Most tabby cat litters have about four kittens.

At birth, tabby kittens are blind and deaf. They drink milk from their mother. When the kittens are two weeks old, their senses begin to function. Soon after, they begin to play and explore. By three weeks, their teeth start coming in. And, they can begin to eat cat food.

Kittens drink milk from their mother until they are about five weeks old.

Each day, the kittens should be gently cuddled. This will create calm, friendly pets. Early handling will also prepare them for grooming. When the kittens are 12 to 16 weeks old, they are ready to go home with new families.

BUYING A KITTEN

So, you have decided to give a tabby cat a home. Good for you! Now you must decide if you want a pet cat or a show cat.

A reputable **breeder** is the best place to look for a show tabby. You could find a show-quality Persian or Maine coon cat. The cost of a show cat will depend on the breed's color and **pedigree**. A kitten that comes from award-winning parents can be very expensive.

If a certain breed is not important to you, visit your local animal shelter or rescue organization. There, lots of tabby cats wait for loving forever homes.

Tabby cats make great companions!

When choosing a tabby kitten or cat, check it closely for signs of good health. Its ears, nose, mouth, and fur should be clean. Its eyes should be bright and clear. The tabby you choose will be a loving family member for 10 to 15 years.

GLOSSARY

breed - a group of animals sharing the same ancestors and appearance. A breeder is a person who raises animals. Raising animals is often called breeding them.

buff - a light yellow color.

Cat Fanciers' Association - a group that sets the standards for judging all breeds of cats.

domestic - tame, especially relating to animals.

Felidae (FEHL-uh-dee) - the scientific Latin name for the cat family. Members of this family are called felids. They include domestic cats, lions, tigers, leopards, jaguars, cougars, wildcats, lynx, and cheetahs.

litter - all of the kittens born at one time to a mother cat.

litter box - a box filled with cat litter, which is similar to sand. Cats use litter boxes to bury their waste.

neuter (NOO-tuhr) - to remove a male animal's reproductive organs.

nutrient - a substance found in food and used in the body. It promotes growth, maintenance, and repair.

pedigree - a record of an animal's ancestors.

pregnant - having one or more babies growing within the body.

purebred - an animal whose parents are both from the same breed.

spay - to remove a female animal's reproductive organs.

ticked - having hair banded with two or more colors. Ticked markings are called ticking.

vaccine (vak-SEEN) - a shot given to prevent illness or disease.

WEB SITES

To learn more about tabby cats, visit ABDO Publishing Company on the World Wide Web at **www.abdopublishing.com**. Web sites about tabby cats are featured on our Book Links page. These links are routinely monitored and updated to provide the most current information available.

INDEX

A

adoption 19, 20, 21
Africa 4, 6

B

body 10, 12
breeder 20

C

care 14, 15, 16, 17,
   19
Cat Fanciers'
   Association 9
character 8, 9, 19,
   21
claws 14, 15
coat 6, 8, 9, 10, 11,
   14, 21
color 6, 8, 9, 10,
   11, 12, 20

E

ears 21
eyes 11, 21

F

face 10
Felidae (family) 4
food 14, 16, 17, 18

G

grooming 14, 19

H

health 14, 15, 16,
   17, 21
history 4, 6
hunting 8, 9, 14, 15

K

kittens 18, 19, 20,
   21

L

life span 21
litter box 14

M

mouth 21

N

neuter 15
nose 21

R

reproduction 18

S

scratching post 15
senses 18
size 12, 17
spay 15

T

tail 10
teeth 18
toys 15

V

vaccines 15
veterinarian 15, 17

W

water 14, 17
wildcat 4, 6, 14

24

DL
2023